Introduction

I learned hand embroidery at an early age—and I still remember my first project, a stamped cross stitch of Donald Duck. Fortunately, my embroidery adventures have progressed from that humble start.

In many ways, hand embroidery is the perfect craft. The supplies are mostly inexpensive and readily available. The options for patterns and thread colors seem limitless. The basic stitches are easily mastered, but the possibilities of stitch variations and skill levels are great, so there is always opportunity to stretch and learn. It is very portable, and you can pick it up and work on it whenever you have a few minutes. And most importantly, there is something very relaxing and satisfying in the process.

I have designed the patterns in this book for both the absolute beginner and for those who need a little refresher course. I chose 10 stitches that are basic but versatile, and designed 11 sewing projects to introduce the stitches. In addition to the 11 projects, there is a sampler wall hanging.

Embroidery is a very old and traditional craft that adapts well to contemporary styles and needs. I hear often that "embroidery is back!" I don't think it was ever really gone, but it is definitely attracting lots of attention these days. It's here, it's updated and it's fun!

Chris Malone

Meet the Designer

Chris Malone has been sewing and crafting most of her life. She has had hundreds of designs published in sewing and quilting publications and has authored several books of her own. She resides in the diverse and beautiful Willamette Valley in Oregon.

Table of Contents

Flutterby Butterfly Fabric Box,
page 24

Embroidery Necessities

You probably already have most of the necessary supplies for hand embroidery if you have basic sewing tools and supplies. There are some wonderful new threads and some interesting new tools on the market today for hand embroidery, but the basic needs are simple: needle, thread, cloth, something to use to transfer the pattern onto the fabric and a sewing machine to complete the projects.

Let's explore some of the products available in these categories and how to choose what best meets your personal requirements. Check the Sources section on page 47 for information on where to purchase these supplies.

Hand Embroidery Threads

Whatever threads you choose to embroider with, always buy good quality because you want something strong and colorfast for all your lovely work.

Stranded Cotton Floss

Embroidery floss is inexpensive, widely available in a myriad of colors and easy to use. It comes in a *skein, a coil of thread or yarn*, and has six strands bundled together that can be divided so that you can stitch a thin or thick line. Most embroidery is worked with two or three strands or just one for fine detail.

To use stranded embroidery floss, cut off an 18-inch length from the skein and slowly pull one strand from the bundle. Pull off as many strands as required, one at a time. Then recombine them and thread them through the needle. This process results in a flatter, smoother stitch than just pulling 2 or 3 strands off the bundle at once.

Pearl Cotton

Pearl (or perle) cotton is a non-separating, twisted thread with a pleasant sheen. It comes in a variety of thicknesses; the lower the number, the heavier the thread. Size 8 is probably easiest for a beginner to use and is comparable to two strands of cotton floss. Sizes 5, 12 and the newer 16 are also useful to collect for creating different looks.

Cotton Petites

Cotton Petites™ is a new product that comes on a spool, so it is easy to use and stores neatly. It is a 12-weight cotton thread, available in lots of colors. One strand equals two strands of embroidery floss.

Other embroidery fibers on the market include wool, rayon, silk, metallic and more, but they are a little more difficult to use and are not featured in the projects in this book.

Needles

A good needle for embroidery has a very sharp point to pierce the fabric and an elongated eye to accommodate the threads. Buy a package of good quality assorted crewel or embroidery needles; the higher the needle number, the finer the needle. If you have trouble threading your needle, try a larger size (smaller number).

An inexpensive needle threader is a good purchase. It has a wire loop that you push through the needle eye. You can easily insert the threads through the loop and then carefully pull the loop back out of the eye, and it will pull the thread with it.

Fabrics

You can embroider on just about anything you can get a needle through, but most stitchers prefer good quality woven cottons and linens or woven or felted wool.

The projects in this book include embroidery on cottons, recycled denim and wool felt. If the item you are embroidering is going to be washed, you should prewash the fabric.

Design Transfer Tools & Techniques

Before you start your embroidery project, you need to transfer the design onto your fabric. Try each transfer tool and technique, weigh their pros and cons, and then choose what works best for you.

Light Box

A light box is a great help when tracing embroidery designs directly onto light-colored fabrics. A window on a sunny day is a good substitute if you don't have a light box. Just tape the design to the light box or window, cover with the fabric, taping it in place, and trace with one of the pens or pencils described below.

Air- & Water-Soluble Pens

Lines marked with these inexpensive pens will come out when washed or just spritzed with water.

Always test these pens on your fabric before using them. Sometimes it can be difficult to completely remove the lines.

Never iron your work until you have completely removed any marks. Heat can set the marks and make them permanent. Even the heat of a light box can set them if you leave it on too long. I know this because it happened to me. I didn't realize it until all the embroidery was complete and I found I could not remove the lines that were not covered by stitches (and I do tend to ad-lib a bit with my designs).

Another disadvantage of these types of marking pens is that they fade, sometimes before you can finish your work, so you may have to re-mark areas.

Permanent Pen

Permanent ink pens, like the popular Micro Pigma, come in colors and very fine tips. They do a nice job of making a clear, fine line to follow, but it is permanent, so you have to completely cover the lines with your embroidery or the lines will show.

Iron-On Transfer Pencils

To use these pencils for transferring, trace the design onto tracing paper. Then place the paper on top of the fabric, marked side of the paper to the right side of fabric, and iron the paper. The design will transfer to the fabric, just like using a purchased iron-on design.

This method can be useful for thicker fabrics that you cannot see through to trace on directly, but the lines are permanent and the design has to be reversed before tracing.

Heat-Sensitive Pens

Heat-sensitive pens like the FriXion pen by Pilot are a recent addition to the market. They come in several colors and write just like a regular ballpoint pen. The marks do not fade and are easily removed with heat—just a touch of an iron or hair dryer takes the marks off.

The marks are "dormant," however, and will return if the fabric is exposed to very cold conditions. This can be an advantage if you accidentally iron your piece prematurely—just pop it in the freezer to restore the lines!

The chemical can be washed out as well. Since this is such a new product and no one knows yet what, if any, damage may result from having fabric exposed to this chemical for a long time, I would not recommend using it to embroider an heirloom christening dress. But for everyday use it is a wonderful tool!

Mechanical Chalk Pencils

A slightly more expensive alternative, mechanical chalk pencils, such as the Bohin brand, come with waxy chalk cartridges in several colors. These pencils make a very fine line (.9mm) which is both washable and erasable using the fabric eraser that comes with the pencil.

Transfer, Graphite or Dressmaker's Carbon Paper

These products come in tissue-like sheets with color on one side. To use them for transferring designs, place the fabric on a smooth, hard surface. Top with the paper, color side down, and then the design. Use a stylus or ballpoint pen to trace over the lines, which will then transfer to the fabric.

The sheets come in different colors, including white for marking dark fabrics. They are easy to use and you do not have to reverse the design. The lines can be rinsed out. Remove the marks completely before ironing.

Tissue Paper

To me, this is a last-resort method that I only use to transfer designs to thick and/or textured dark fabrics that would be difficult to mark with any of the other methods. It is fairly time-consuming but it leaves no marks on the fabric and is accurate.

Trace your design onto tissue paper and baste this paper onto the right side of your fabric. Embroider through the tissue paper and fabric, following the pattern lines. When finishing, carefully tear away the tissue paper, using tweezers to remove any little bits that remain.

Cardstock Templates

This is a method that I use occasionally when I can't see through my fabric to trace and only when the embroidery design is simple.

Trace the motif onto paper, adhere this paper to cardstock and cut out. Place the template onto the fabric and trace around it with one of the transfer pens.

Other Tools & Aids

Sharp Scissors

You'll need small scissors for snipping threads and larger scissors for cutting the fabric. To keep them sharp, do not use them for cutting anything but fibers. Cutting paper dulls scissors quickly.

Embroidery Hoops

A hoop is used to maintain a good, even tension when stitching. It holds the fabric taut and most people find that it makes embroidery easier. Some, however, feel that a hoop gets in the way and prefer to stitch without one. I nearly always use a hoop, except when stitching on felt or other thick materials.

Hoops now come in plastic and wood (the old metal hoops have a tendency to leave stains on the fabric).

To use a hoop, place the fabric over the inner (small) ring and then attach the outer ring by pushing it over the edges of the inner ring. If necessary, turn the tension knob to enlarge the outer ring and then tighten it again when the fabric is in place.

If possible, use a hoop that contains the entire design. If the design is large, work one section and then move the hoop to prepare the next area. Two sizes of hoops will meet most of your needs: a 4- or 5-inch hoop is good for most small projects and an 8-inch hoop for larger designs.

Lightweight Fusible Interfacing

Fusing a piece of lightweight interfacing to the back of a design gives the fabric more body and stability and makes it easier to maintain an even tension while stitching, especially if not using a hoop. In addition, it helps to hide the knots and any traveling threads on the back.

Fuse the interfacing before tracing the design if you are using a pen with ink that either erases with heat or that sets with heat!

Use interfacing when working a padded satin stitch. Cut out the motif shape and fuse it to the right side of the fabric. Stitch over it to achieve a slightly dimensional effect.

Doodle Cloth

It is nice to have a cloth handy to audition a new stitch or thread before committing it to a project. Use a fabric similar to what you will be working on and just play with it. You can use a fabric pen to jot the stitch name and threads used so it becomes a permanent stitch journal.

Good Lighting

This is so important (and the older your eyes are, the more it helps!). Use daylight rated bulbs in lamps placed behind your left shoulder if you are right-handed.

Iron, Ironing Board & Towel

Pad your ironing board with a towel before pressing your completed stitchery to avoid flattening the stitches.

Choose a heat setting suitable to both the fabric and thread. If several temperatures apply, always use the lowest setting.

Place the completed piece facedown on the padded ironing surface. Cover the piece with a lightweight, white damp cloth.

Lightly press the embroidered area by lifting and replacing the iron in a new area. Never drag the iron across the embroidered area.

Lay work flat to dry completely.

Basic General Sewing Supplies & Tools

We have provided a wide range of projects, from sweet to whimsical, traditional to contemporary, and from very easy to a bit more complicated to showcase your embroidery skills. Check your general sewing supplies against this basic sewing supply list to have what you will need to complete the projects.

Basic Sewing Supplies & Equipment

- Sewing machine in good working order with zigzag or overedge stitch capability.
    A walking foot is helpful for stitching through multiple layers.
- Matching all-purpose thread
- Hand-sewing needles and thimble
- Straight pins and pincushion
- Seam ripper
- Removable fabric marking pens or tailor's chalk
- Measuring tools:
    tape measure
    variety clear sewing rulers
- Pattern tracing paper or cloth
- Point turner
- Pressing equipment:
    steam iron and ironing board
    press cloths
- Scissors:
    fabric shears
    pinking shears
    paper scissors
- Seam sealant or no-fray solution

Optional Supplies & Equipment

- Serger
- Fabric glue
- Fabric spray adhesive
- Rotary cutter, mats and straightedges
- Pressing hams/sleeve rolls

Stitch Guide

There are so many documented embroidery stitches to work with. I have selected 10 fundamental and versatile stitches (and a few fun variations of some of the stitches) that I think will provide a good start to learning this craft. The following stitch guide describes the stitches in detail.

Practice the stitches on your doodle cloth, then check out the included projects for embroidery designs utilizing these stitches. Each project highlights a new stitch leading up to a grand finale sampler showing off all the stitches in a colorful wall hanging.

Full-size embroidery designs are included on the insert for each of the projects. Refer to the project photos, the colored individual designs and the embroidery instructions included with each project to stitch them like the samples.

Running Stitches

The running stitch is a simple, multipurpose stitch. It is the basis of any hand sewing, because a line of running stitches can be used to seam layers of fabric together. A running stitch becomes a gathering stitch if you pull on a thread end. As an embroidery stitch, it can be used for lines, to outline a shape and to give texture and interest to a shape.

Running Stitch

• Run the needle in and out of the fabric at regular intervals.

• The whipped running stitch variation is made by whipping or weaving a second thread through a line of running stitches on the top of the fabric, not piercing the fabric.

Whipped Running Stitch

You can use the same thread, which results in a nice textured outline, or a contrasting thread for an accent.

Use a tapestry needle, which has a blunt end instead of a sharp point, or just use the eye part of the embroidery needle to whip or weave the second thread so you don't catch the fabric.

Backstitch

The backstitch, a very useful and beautiful stitch, is used to outline shapes, even on small motifs. If a shape is complex, just make the stitches small so they stay on the design lines. Backstitch is also good for lettering.

• Bring the needle and thread up at 1. Take a small backstitch to 2, and then bring it out again, one stitch length ahead of 1 at 3.

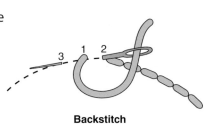

Backstitch

The space between 1 and 2 and between 2 and 3 should be the same. Continue to make backstitches into the hole of the previous stitch.

A backstitch variation is used to attach beads to fabric. This backstitch beading technique can be used to add single beads or multiple beads to a design.

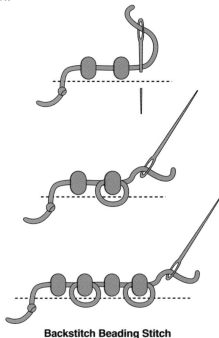

Backstitch Beading Stitch

• Use a doubled length of sewing thread that coordinates with the bead color. Bring the needle up at the beginning of the beaded line, slip two beads onto the needle, and lay them down on the line. Take the needle back down into the fabric, right next to the second bead.

Bring the needle up again between the two beads and take the needle back through the second bead again.

Pick up two more beads, lay them down on the line, and go back into the fabric. Come up again between the third and fourth bead. Repeat this process of picking up beads and backstitching to keep the row of beads secure and in a straight line. Knot and clip the thread close to secure the end of the beaded line.

Stem or Outline Stitches

The stem and outline stitches are used to outline shapes and make bold lines. They can also be used to fill in shapes by working rows close together, as in crewel work.

Though the names stem and outline stitches are often used interchangeably, there actually is a distinction. When making the stem stitch, the thread is kept below the needle insertions. When making an outline stitch, the thread is kept above the needle insertions.

Any of the patterns in this book that call for a stem or outline stitch can be worked either way. It is important to keep the stitches consistent. So be careful to not mix the stem and outline stitches on the same stitching line.

• For the stem stitch, bring the needle and thread up at 1 and insert the needle at 2. Keeping the thread down, bring the

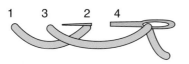

Stem Stitch

needle back up at 3 (halfway between 1 and 2). Insert the needle at 4 and bring it back out at the end of 2. Continue on the line, always bringing the needle out in the hole of the previous stitch.

• The outline stitch is made in the same manner, but the thread is kept above the needle.

Outline Stitch

• The alternating stem stitch mixes the stem and outline stitches. Instead of consistently holding the

Alternating Stem Stitch

thread above or below the needle, the thread is held below for the first stitch, above for the second, below for the third and so on. It makes an interesting thick stitch with lots of texture.

Knot Stitches

Knots are fun, dimensional stitches often used for dots, eyes, flower centers or just as a decorative accent.

The French knot and the colonial knot (also called the figure-eight knot or candlewicking knot) are made just a little bit differently, but look very much alike when they are finished. Since they can be used interchangeably, try them both to discover which one is easier for you.

French Knot

• To make a French knot, bring the needle and thread up at 1. Hold the thread taut and wrap it around the needle twice, then pull it gently to keep the wraps snug but not too tight. Keeping the tension, insert the needle back into the fabric at 2, about one thread away from 1. Push the loops down the needle to lie on top of the fabric, and then pull the needle through carefully.

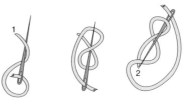

Colonial Knot

• To make a colonial knot, bring the needle and thread up at 1. Take the thread over and under the needle, then over the needle again in the opposite direction to form a figure eight. Tip the needle back toward the fabric and insert the tip into the fabric at 2 about one thread away from 1. Pull the thread to make the wraps snug but not too tight. Push the loops down the needle to lie on top of the fabric, and carefully pull the needle through.

8

Lazy Daisy Stitch

The lazy daisy stitch is also known as the detached chain stitch. If you make one chain stitch and end it with a small stitch at the tip to secure it, you have a lazy daisy stitch.

The lazy daisy stitch is used most often to make flower petals and little leaves. If you leave the stitches loose, you will make fatter loops; if you pull the stitches tighter, you will have straighter, thinner loops.

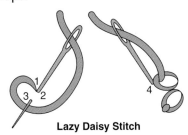

Lazy Daisy Stitch

- Bring the needle and thread up at 1. Holding the thread down with the thumb of your non-needle hand, insert the needle into 2, next to 1, and come up at 3, over the loop of thread. Insert the needle directly below 3, at 4, to secure and complete the stitch.

Chain Stitches

The chain stitch is a line of closed-looped stitches that forms a chain-like pattern. Chain stitches are quick to work and can be used to outline shapes or follow straight or curved lines, including lettering. Worked in close rows, it can be used for a filling stitch as well.

Chain Stitch

- This stitch starts the same as a lazy daisy stitch. Bring the needle up at 1, hold the thread down and insert the needle at 2, next to 1. Bring it back up at 3, pull the thread through, and start a new loop.

Zigzag Chain Stitch

There are many variations of this decorative stitch. Try alternating a short stitch with a long stitch, or work stitches in a zigzag pattern, which resembles a line of rickrack. This zigzag stitch is made just like the regular chain stitch, but at alternating angles.

Fly Stitch

The fly stitch is also sometimes called the Y stitch (because it looks like a Y!). It's one of my favorite stitches because it works so well for leaf centers and vines. The stitch can be worked in single detached units, horizontally or vertically. The anchoring stitch (3–4) can be short or long, so there are lots of variations to play with.

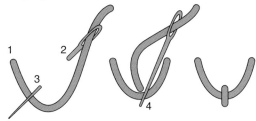

Fly Stitch

- Bring the needle and thread up at 1 and insert at 2, directly across from 1. Bring the needle back up at 3, which is below and centered between 1 and 2. Take the needle down at 4 to finish the stitch.

Fly Stitch Variation

- To embroider a leaf center or a vine, start with a straight stitch down the line, and then make a fly stitch. Repeat fly stitches down the pattern line, ending with a straight stitch.

Blanket Stitches

The blanket stitch or open buttonhole stitch is probably one that you see often. It is used as a border stitch, a decorative stitch to finish edges, and as a way to attach appliqué shapes to the background fabric. It is also used frequently to sew two layers of fabric together along the edges, especially felt or felted wool. When the looped stitches are worked very close together, it is called a buttonhole stitch.

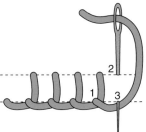

Blanket Stitch

• Bring the needle and thread up at 1. *If you are appliquéing a shape to the background, 1 will be on the background, next to the edge of the appliqué.* Hold the thread down with the thumb of your non-needle hand and insert the needle at 2, which is over and above 1 *(and inside the appliqué edge)*. Bring needle back up at 3, which is directly under 2, with the working thread under the needle tip. Repeat to make the next stitch.

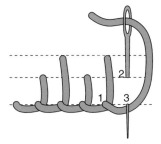

Blanket Stitch Variation

The variations on the blanket stitch seem endless. For example, you can vary the length of the stitches and the distance between the stitches to create different patterns. One variation is to work the blanket stitch in the normal manner, but vary the length of the 2-3 stitch: short, tall, short, tall.

Satin Stitches

The satin stitch is a filling stitch used to create a smooth "satiny" surface. It consists of straight stitches worked side by side, closely together. The object is to fill a shape completely without leaving spaces or letting the stitches stack up or form a bumpy surface.

The satin stitch is not meant to cover large areas; a stitch length of 1½ inches is about the length limit. If the stitches are too long, they tend to catch on things and fray. You can start at one end of the shape and work across or start in the middle and work to both sides.

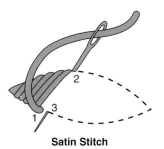

Satin Stitch

• Start at one side of the motif and bring the needle up at 1. Take the stitch back down at 2, across the shape. Come up again at 3, a thread or two away from 1, to make the next stitch. Take the stitches across from side to side, keeping them even and closely spaced. This stitch can be made horizontally, vertically or diagonally.

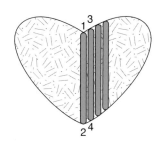

**Padded Satin Stitch
With Underlay**

• For a raised effect, you can work a padded satin stitch in several easy ways. I like to cut the shape out of lightweight interfacing and fuse it in place. Then follow the edge of the interfacing for stitch placement.

For an even more raised effect, use a piece of fusible web and fabric or felt in the color of the thread you will be using. Fuse the cutout to the background and satin stitch over it.

A third technique is to outline the shape with a backstitch or outline stitch and work the satin stitches over the edge of the outline.

Cross Stitches

When most people hear the words cross stitch, they think of counted cross stitch where the stitches are placed and made by counting the threads on even-weave fabrics. Some cross stitch designs are extremely detailed and elaborate.

But the humble cross stitch is a cute little stitch all on its own and can be used for a pretty filling stitch or a precise border.

It is a very simple stitch to make. There are two methods of working the cross stitch. You can work a row of half stitches, then work back, crossing the half stitch lines. Or you can complete each X as you go. The first method works best for horizontal rows of cross stitches and the second method is better for vertical rows or scattered, single cross stitches.

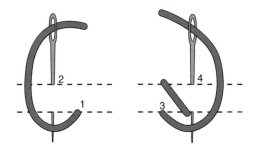

Single Cross-Stitch

• Bring the needle and thread up at 1. Take a diagonal stitch down at 2 and come up at 3. Take a diagonal stitch back down at 4.

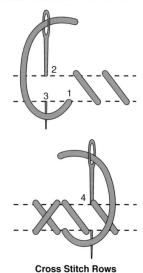

Cross Stitch Rows

• Work a row of half stitches, coming up at 1 and down at 2. Work in the opposite direction from the end of the row, coming up at 3 and down at 4 and crossing over the first stitches.

The double cross stitch is a fun variation to try. Make one cross stitch and then add a second one on top, at a 45-degree angle, to form a star.

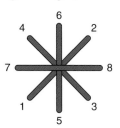

Double Cross Stitch

• Complete a single cross stitch. Come up again at 5 and make a stitch across and down at 6. Come up at 7 and make a final stitch to 8 to form a star.

Make a flower using an easy variation of the double cross stitch by sewing four straight stitches at the ends of the points.

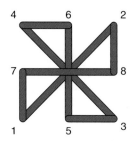

Double Cross Stitch Flower

• Make a double cross stitch star and make four straight stitches connecting the points. Bring needle up at 4, stitch down at 6, up at 2 and down at 8, up at 3 and down at 5, and finally up at 1 and down at 7. ❖

Soft & Sweet Needle Book & Pincushion

This little set, made with wool felt and featuring the running stitch, will be a good addition to your sewing basket. The needle book has several pages, so it is easy to keep your needles sorted by size.

Finished Sizes

Needle Book: 4½ x 4½ inches (closed)

Pincushion: 5 x 5 inches

Materials

Materials are listed for both Needle Book and Pincushion.
- Wool felt* (36-inch-wide or 9 x 12-inch craft sheets):
    ¼ yard or 2 sheets gray tonal
    ¼ yard or 1 sheet white
    ⅛ yard or 1 sheet soft green
- Size 8 pearl cotton: white, soft green
- Buttons:
    2 (⅜-inch diameter) pink shank
    1 (¾-inch diameter) pink shank
    4 (⅜-inch diameter) flat white pearl
- ¾ yard ½-inch-wide pink wire-edge ribbon
- Cotton stuffing
- Fabric glue
- Freezer paper (optional)
- Basic sewing supplies and equipment
*Good quality acrylic felt can be substituted for wool felt.

Cutting

From gray felt:
- Cut 2 (4½ x 9¼-inch) rectangles for needle book cover.
- Cut 2 (5 x 5-inch) squares for pincushion front/back.

From white felt:
- Cut 2 (4 x 8¾-inch) rectangles with pinking shears for needle book pages.
- For needle book flowers, cut 1 each 5 x ¾-inch and 4½ x ⅝-inch strips. Cut one long edge and both short ends of strips with pinking shears.
- For pincushion flower, cut 1 (9 x 1¼-inch) strip. Cut one long edge and both short ends with pinking shears.

From soft green felt:
- Using templates provided on insert, cut 1 double stem, 1 single stem and 7 leaves.

Cutting Tip

An easy and accurate method of cutting shapes from felt or fabric is to trace the pattern onto the nonwaxed side of freezer paper, leaving a small margin around each shape. Cut the shapes apart and iron the waxed side to the felt or wrong side of the fabric (about three seconds). The paper will stick to the felt. Cut out each shape on the pattern lines and remove the paper.

Needle Book Assembly

1. To make the felt flowers, thread a needle with a double strand of white sewing thread and knot. Stitch a ¼-inch-long running stitch ⅛ inch up from the bottom straight edge (Figure 1).

Figure 1

2. Pull the thread to tightly gather the edge. Knot and clip the thread close to the knot. Repeat with the remaining strip.

3. Arrange the double stem and two leaf appliqué pieces on the right half of one needle book cover rectangle (Figure 2).

Figure 2

4. Use a length of soft green pearl cotton to stitch a running stitch up the center of the stem appliqué and around the edges of the leaves.

5. Apply a few dots of fabric glue to the back gathered section of the larger flower and press to the top of the longer stem section, referring to Figure 3. Insert and stitch the shank of a ⅜-inch pink button into the hole of the flower. Repeat with the smaller flower and remaining stem.

Figure 3

6. Center the ribbon on the wrong side of remaining cover rectangle (Figure 4). Use small dots of glue to secure.

Figure 4

7. Pin cover rectangles wrong sides together. Stitch a running stitch in white pearl cotton ⅛ inch from all edges. *Note: Be sure to stitch through the ribbon to secure.*

8. Stitch a running stitch around each of the four leaves using one length of green pearl cotton.

9. Apply a few dots of fabric glue to the back of a leaf and press it to the top right corner of a white page rectangle. Turn the page over and lightly glue a leaf to the bottom left corner.

10. Repeat step 9 with the remaining leaves and white page rectangle. Sew a pearl button to the base of each leaf (Figure 5).

Figure 5

11. Starting near the leaf and leaving a 4-inch tail, stitch a running stitch ³⁄₁₆ inch from page edges using green pearl cotton.

12. When you reach the starting point, tie the threads into a knot and then in a bow (Figure 6). Trim the tails to 1½ inches. Apply a dot of seam sealant to the ends of the pearl cotton and at the bow center to secure it.

Figure 6

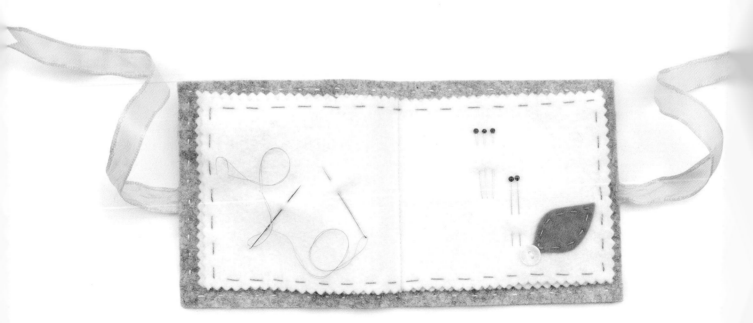

13. Stack and center the page rectangles on the inside of the needle book cover. Machine-stitch all layers through the vertical center of the cover and pages, referring to Figure 7.

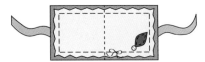

Figure 7

14. Fold the book in half on the stitched line and tie the ribbon into a bow to close. Trim the ribbon ends as desired and apply seam sealant to the cut ends.

Soft & Sweet Needle Book & Pincushion
Needle Book Placement Diagram
9¼" x 4½" Finished

Pincushion Assembly

1. Follow steps 1 and 2 of the Needle Book assembly instructions using the 9 x 1¼-inch strip to make a flower.

2. Arrange the single stem and a leaf near the top left corner of one of the 5-inch gray squares. Stitch a running stitch up the center of the stem and around the leaf using green pearl cotton.

3. Referring to Figure 3 and step 5 of Needle Book Assembly, apply a few dots of fabric glue to the back gathered section of the felt flower and press it to the tip of the stem. Insert the shank of the ¾-inch pink button into the hole of the flower and stitch in place.

Assembly Tip
Use liquid fabric glue sparingly. Too much glue and the felt or fabric will be stiff when dried.
A small dot of glue is more than enough.

4. Pin the pincushion squares wrong sides together and stitch a running stitch ¼ inch from the outside edges. Hide the beginning knot between the layers.

5. Stop stitching about 2 inches from the first stitch. Insert stuffing into the pincushion. Complete the running stitches and hide the ending knot between the layers. ❖

Soft & Sweet Needle Book & Pincushion
Pincushion Placement Diagram
5" x 5" Finished

Cuppa Coaster Set

This little set of coasters is a good project for practicing the backstitch. Choose border fabrics that coordinate with your home decor or make them as a special gift.

Finished Size
5 x 5 inches

Materials
- ⅛ yard each orange, green, turquoise and purple prints
- ¼ yard or fat quarter tan solid or tonal
- 12 x 23-inch piece cotton batting
- Stranded embroidery floss to match fabrics:
  - medium brown   light brown
  - orange   green
  - turquoise   purple
- Basic sewing supplies and equipment

Cutting

From each color print:
- Cut 2 each 1 x 4½-inch and 1 x 5½-inch border strips.
- Cut 1 (5½-inch) backing square.

From cotton batting:
- Cut 8 (5½-inch) squares.

Embroidery
Refer to Embroidery Necessities on page 2 for stitching tips and the Stitch Guide on page 6. Full-size embroidery design is included on the insert.

1. Mark four 4½-inch squares on right side of tan fabric, leaving a margin of about 2 inches around the squares; do not cut out. *Note: You can cut off any excess yardage, but leave enough fabric to use a hoop if desired.*

2. Transfer a cup embroidery design to each square using your preferred transfer method.

3. Use 3 strands of floss and the backstitch to embroider the cup pattern on one of the marked squares as follows: cup outline, brown; cup stripe, orange and steam lines, light brown. Repeat with each of the remaining squares, using either green, turquoise or purple floss for the cup stripes.

4. Remove any visible pattern lines; cut out each 4½-inch square and press.

Assembly
Use ¼-inch seam allowance and stitch right sides together unless otherwise indicated.

1. Stitch a 1 x 4½-inch green strip to opposite sides of the green-striped cup embroidery square (Figure 1). Press seams toward the border.

Figure 1

2. Stitch a 1 x 5½-inch green strip to the top and bottom of the embroidered square, referring again to Figure 1; press seams toward the border.

3. Repeat steps 1 and 2 with the remaining embroidered squares, matching the border strips to the color of the cup stripe.

4. Layer two batting squares, an embroidered/bordered square, right side up, and a backing square, right side down. Stitch all around leaving a 2½-inch opening on one side. Trim corners at an angle. Trim batting close to seam.

5. Turn coaster right side out through opening, carefully poking out corners. Fold opening seam allowance to inside and press coaster edges flat. Slip stitch opening closed.

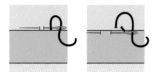

Slip Stitch

6. Stitch-in-the-ditch around the coaster at the border seam.

7. Using 3 strands of floss matching the stripe and border fabric, stitch a running stitch ¼ inch from the border seam through all layers to quilt the coaster layers, referring to Figure 2.

¼"

Figure 2

8. Repeat steps 4–8 to make one coaster each with orange, green, turquoise and purple borders and backing. ❖

Cheery Cherry Tea Towel Set

Tea towels make great gifts. They come in wonderful colors and are fun to embroider. Embellish them even more with a fabric ruffle. This set features the stem or outline stitch.

Finished Size
Size of purchased towel, about 18 x 28 inches

Materials
Materials listed make a set of two tea towels.

- ⅛ yard red and cream plaid
- ¼ yard green and cream stripe
- 2 green purchased tea towels
- Stranded embroidery floss:
  red   dark green
  brown   tan
  cream
- Basic sewing supplies and equipment

Cutting

From plaid:
- Cut 2 (2-inch x width of towel plus ½ inch) strips for ruffle band.

From stripe:
- Cut 2 (2½ x 42-inch) ruffle strips.

Embroidery
Refer to Embroidery Necessities on page 2 for stitching tips and the Stitch Guide on page 6. Full-size embroidery designs are included on the insert.

1. Prewash and press purchased tea towels.

2. Use your preferred method to transfer either the cherry or pie embroidery designs centered 3½ inches up from the bottom edge of each towel.

3. Embroider the cherries and pie, using either a stem stitch or an outline stitch and 2 strands of floss as follows:

Cherries and pie pan	red
Leaves	dark green
Stems	brown
Pastry	tan
Steam lines	cream

Assembly

Use ¼-inch seam allowance and stitch right sides together unless otherwise indicated.

1. Machine-stitch a ¼-inch double turned hem on both short ends and one long edge of each ruffle strip.

2. Machine-stitch two rows of gathering stitches ¼ and ³⁄₁₆ inch from the raw edge of each ruffle strip (Figure 1).

Figure 1

3. Gather both ruffle strips to match the width of the towel and tie off gathering thread ends.

4. Mark a line 1 inch up from the bottom on the right side of a towel. Position and pin a ruffle, right side up, with the raw edge along the marked line (Figure 2).

Figure 2

5. Machine-stitch the ruffle, ¼ inch from the ruffle raw edge, to the towel.

6. Fold and press the short ends of the plaid ruffle band ¼ inch to wrong side. Then fold and press the strip in half lengthwise, wrong sides together (Figure 3).

Figure 3

7. Position and pin the band on the ruffle, matching the raw edges, and stitch (Figure 4).

Figure 4

the raw edges, and pin. Topstitch close to the band edges all around to finish (Figure 5).

Figure 5

8. Press the band away from the ruffle, covering

9. Repeat steps 4–8 to complete the second towel. ❖

Magnetic Personality

This is a quick and easy project and a good way to practice knots. You can try other combinations of stitches too—just draw circles on a piece of paper and design your own patterns!

Finished Size
1½-inch diameter

Materials
- Scraps yellow, red and black solids
- Lightweight fusible interfacing
- Size 8 pearl cotton:
  - yellow   red
  - black   white
- 3 (1½-inch-diameter) cover button kits
- 3 (¾-inch-diameter) magnets
- Metal glue (optional)
- Basic sewing supplies and equipment

Embroidery
Refer to Embroidery Necessities on page 2 for stitching tips and the Stitch Guide on page 6. Full-size embroidery designs are included on the insert.

1. Draw three 2⅝-inch diameter circles on the non-glue side of the fusible interfacing, leaving a small space between each circle.

2. Cut the circles apart and follow the manufacturer's directions to fuse one circle to the wrong side of each yellow, red and black fabric scrap. Cut out each circle on the pattern lines.

3. Transfer the embroidery designs centered on the fabric and embroider the circles using 1 strand of pearl cotton:

Red Circle

Make eight black straight stitches radiating out from the center with a yellow French knot or colonial knot at the end of each stitch and a black knot in the center. Stitch a white running stitch around the edges.

Yellow Circle

Stitch a black running stitch in an even grid. Make alternating red and white knots in each square.

Black Circle

Backstitch the small circle in yellow. Stitch a red running stitch around the edge. Make a center white knot and white knots spaced evenly between the yellow and red circles.

Assembly
1. Remove the wire shank from the cover buttons.

2. Stitch a running stitch around the edge of an embroidered circle. Center the button on the wrong side of the circle and pull the thread to gather the edges. Check the front and re-center the button if necessary. Snap the button back in place, following the manufacturer's directions.

3. Repeat with the remaining embroidered circles and buttons.

4. If using adhesive backed magnets, remove the paper backing from the foam adhesive and press a magnet to the back of each button. If using plain magnets, use a metal glue to attach the magnets. ❖

Embroidery Tip
You shouldn't need a hoop for this embroidery since the interfacing stabilizes the fabric and the piece is quite small.

If you prefer a hoop, use a large enough scrap to fit the hoop and draw one or all of the circles on the right side of the fabric corresponding to the circles on the interfacing to position the embroidery pattern.

Sweet Kitty Pincushion

This whimsical cat pincushion has a trio of embroidered flowers made with lazy daisy stitches. She stands upright, ready to hold pins and needles for your sewing projects.

Finished Size
4 x 6 inches

Materials
- Scrap pink print
- ¼ yard or fat quarter gray check
- Size 8 pearl cotton:
    light pink
    dark pink
    green
    yellow
    black
- Size 16 (or 12) black pearl cotton
- Buttons:
    2 (¼-inch-diameter) black
    1 (⁷⁄₁₆-inch-diameter) pink
- 12 inches 1½-inch-wide pink check wire-edge ribbon
- Scrap paper-backed fusible web
- Scrap thin batting or polyester fleece
- ½ cup crushed walnut shells
- Fiberfill or cotton stuffing
- Basic sewing supplies and equipment

Cutting
Full-size templates are included on the insert for body, outer and inner ear, tail and base pieces. Transfer all markings from templates to fabric.

From pink:
- Trace 2 inner ears about ½ inch apart onto paper side of fusible web and cut out. Apply to wrong side of fabric following manufacturer's instructions. Cut out on template lines.

From gray check:
- Cut 1 (8 x 10-inch) rectangle.
- Cut 4 outer ears, 2 tails (reversing one) and 1 each body back and base.

Embroidery
Refer to Embroidery Necessities on page 2 for stitching tips and the Stitch Guide on page 6. Full-size embroidery design is included on the insert.

1. Using embroidery design provided, draw the cat body outline centered on the right side of the gray check 8 x 10-inch rectangle with a pencil.

2. Use your preferred method to transfer the embroidery design onto the cat body.

3. Embroider the design as follows.

Use 1 strand size 8 pearl cotton to stitch:
Stems	green stem/outline stitch
Leaves	green lazy daisy stitch
Center flower	dark pink lazy daisy stitch
Side flowers	light pink lazy daisy stitch
Flower centers	yellow knot
Whiskers	black straight stitch

Use 1 strand size 16 pearl cotton to stitch:
Bee outline	black stem/outline stitch
Bee eye	black knot
Bee trail	black running stitch
Under nose	black stem/outline stitch

Assembly
Use ¼-inch seam allowance and stitch right sides together unless otherwise indicated.

1. Use black sewing thread to sew the black buttons to the face for eyes referring to the embroidery design for placement.

2. Use pink sewing thread to sew the pink button to the face for a nose referring to the embroidery design for placement.

3. Cut the embroidered front out on the template lines.

4. Remove paper backing from inner ear pieces. Center and fuse an inner ear on right side of each outer ear (Figure 1).

Figure 1

5. Layer fused ears right sides together with remaining outer ears and pin to scraps of batting. Stitch around ears leaving flat bottom edge open.

6. Trim batting close to seam, clip curves and trim point. Turn right side out and press flat.

7. Machine-topstitch around the pink inner ear through all layers (Figure 2).

Figure 2

8. Make a tail referring to steps 5 and 6.

9. Pin and baste ears and tail to right side of embroidered body front between placement circles referring to pattern and Figure 3.

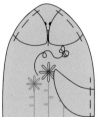

Figure 3

10. Pin body front and back, right sides together, and stitch all around, leaving seam open at straight bottom and between squares on side. Clip the curves. Do not turn right side out.

11. Mark the center front and back of the body. Pin the body to the base, matching centers to squares on base and side seams to circles.

12. Stitch body and base together all around. Clip the curves and turn right side out through the body opening.

13. Pour crushed walnut shells into the body through the opening. Stuff the body firmly with fiberfill or cotton stuffing.

14. Fold opening seam allowance to inside and slip stitch opening closed to complete cat.

15. Tie the ribbon into a bow and trim the ends as desired. Tack the bow to the side of the cat, referring to the sample photo. ❖

Slip Stitch

Flutterby Butterfly Fabric Box

Create a handy little fabric box perfect for corralling your embroidery and sewing supplies. The flower and butterfly are dimensional, and the butterfly wings provide a good surface for the chain stitch in colorful floss.

Finished Size
6 x 6 x 6 inches

Materials
- 10 x 10-inch piece orange solid
- ¼ yard or fat quarter yellow solid
- ¼ yard each turquoise and lime green solids
- ¼ yard fusible fleece
- 10 x 10-inch piece low loft batting or polyester fleece
- Stranded embroidery floss:
  - orange   red   green   turquoise
  - purple   pink   yellow   black
- 5¾-inch square stiff interfacing or plastic canvas
- 1 (⅞-inch-diameter) cover button kit
- 2-inch square lightweight fusible interfacing
- 12 (6mm) black beads
- 6 inches DMC Memory Thread or 18-gauge black wire
- Fabric glue
- Walking foot for sewing machine (optional)
- Basic sewing supplies and equipment

Cutting

From turquoise:
- Cut 2 (6½ x 12½-inch) rectangles for box sides.
- Cut 1 (6½-inch) square for box bottom.

From lime green:
- Cut 2 (6½ x 12½-inch) rectangles for lining sides.
- Cut 1 (6½-inch) square for lining bottom.
- Cut 1 (4 x 25-inch) binding strip.

From fusible fleece:
- Cut 2 (6¼ x 12¼-inch) rectangles.
- Cut 1 (6¼-inch) square.

Box Assembly
Use ¼-inch seam allowance and stitch right sides together unless otherwise indicated. Refer to Embroidery Necessities on page 2 for stitching tips and the Stitch Guide on page 6. Full-size embroidery design and templates are included on the insert.

1. Center and fuse fusible fleece pieces to the wrong side of the turquoise sides and bottom pieces following the manufacturer's instructions.

2. Position the butterfly flight design 4¾ inches from the left side and 1½ inches up from the bottom edge of the right side of a side rectangle, referring to Figure 1 for orientation. Transfer the design using your preferred transfer method.

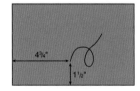

Figure 1

3. Stitch the butterfly flight pattern in a running stitch using 2 strands of black embroidery floss.

4. Pin-mark the center of the bottom long edge of both rectangles and all four sides of the bottom square.

5. Match the center of the embroidered rectangle to the center of one side of the bottom square; pin matching edges.

6. Stitch together, starting and stopping ¼ inch from the corners of the bottom square referring

to (Figure 2); backstitch to secure. Press seam toward bottom square. Repeat with remaining side rectangle to make box unit (Figure 3).

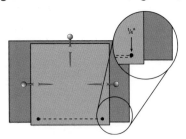

Figure 2

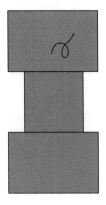

Figure 3

7. Fold box unit in half, matching the short ends of the rectangles. Stitch short ends together (Figure 4). Press seams open. Do not turn right side out.

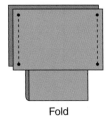

Fold

Figure 4

8. To form the box, fold one side seam down to match the center of a bottom square side (Figure 5). Pin and stitch with bottom side up.

Figure 5

9. Repeat, stitching the opposite side seam and bottom square side (Figure 6). Turn the box right side out. Insert the stiff interfacing or plastic canvas square into the bottom of the box.

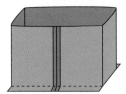

Figure 6

10. Assemble box lining using lime green fabric, referring to steps 4–9. Do not turn right side out.

11. Insert the lining into the box, wrong sides together, matching the side seams and corners. Baste all around the top edge to secure.

12. Measure around the top outside edge of the box and add ½ inch. Trim the binding strip to this total. **Note:** *The sample measured 24 inches. The sample binding strip was trimmed to 24½ inches.*

13. Stitch binding strip short ends together to make a circle; press seam open. Fold and press strip in half lengthwise to 2 inches wide.

14. Slip the binding over the top of the box with binding seam at center back. Match and pin raw edges of binding to top of box. Stitch ½-inch seam allowance all around box top (Figure 7).

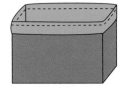

Figure 7

15. Fold the binding folded edge to the inside of the box covering raw edges and seam; pin in place (Figure 8). Slip stitch the folded edge of the binding to the lining, again referring to Figure 8. **Note:** *If desired, machine-stitch just below the seam on the outside of the box through all thicknesses, catching the folded edge of the binding in the stitching.*

Figure 8

16. If desired, fold each corner of the box and steam-press to define the box shape.

Box Embellishment

Refer to Embroidery Necessities on page 2 for stitching tips and the Stitch Guide on page 6. Full-size embroidery design and templates are included on the insert. Use ¼-inch seam allowance and stitch right sides together unless otherwise indicated.

Flower & Leaves

1. Trace the flower petal template four times onto the wrong side of half the orange fabric, leaving at least ½ inch between the shapes.

2. Fold the fabric in half, right sides together with traced shapes on top, and pin to a scrap of batting (Figure 9).

Figure 9

3. Stitch around each petal, leaving open at the bottom straight edge. Cut out ⅛ inch from the seam. Trim the batting close to the seam and clip the curves. Turn each petal right side out and press.

4. To make the leaves, repeat steps 1 and 2, tracing leaf pattern. Stitch completely around leaf shape. Trim batting close to seam, clip curves and trim leaf point.

5. Make a slash through one layer of fabric only (Figure 10). Apply seam sealant to cut edges; let dry. Turn leaves right side out through slash and press. Hand-stitch slash edges together.

Figure 10

6. Stitch a running stitch, through all layers, down the center of each leaf and 3⁄16 inch from the outer edge of each petal and leaf using 2 strands of black floss.

7. Stitch 2–3 running stitches at the base of one petal with a knotted, doubled strand of sewing thread. Pull the thread to gather and then add a second petal. Repeat until all four petals are joined and gathered (Figure 11); knot and clip thread.

Figure 11

8. For the flower center, fuse the square of light-weight fusible interfacing to the wrong side of a yellow fabric scrap. Draw and cut out a 1¾-inch circle. Transfer the flower center embroidery design to the center of the circle. Use 3 strands of yellow floss to make a knot on each dot of the design.

9. Use a doubled strand of sewing thread to stitch running stitches around the outer edge of the embroidered circle. Remove the shank and center the cover button on the wrong side. Pull the thread to gather the edges around the button. Attach the button back following the manufacturer's instructions.

10. Glue the button to the center of the flower petals, covering the raw edges.

11. Apply glue to the back of the flower at the bottom edge of the petals. Press flower to the lower front left corner of the box.

12. Apply glue to the back of each leaf at the base end only. Tuck the leaves behind the flower, referring to the project photo.

Butterfly

1. Cut an 8-inch square of yellow fabric and trace butterfly template onto the center.

2. Transfer the butterfly embroidery design onto the right side of the yellow using your preferred transfer method.

3. Use 3 strands of floss to stitch the butterfly embroidery stitches as follows:

• Chain stitch the upper oval spot with two lines of orange and red.

• Chain stitch the lower spots with two lines of turquoise and purple.

• Stitch pink knots in a circle for the inside of the upper ovals.

• Stitch five single green knots down the center of each lower oval.

• Sew three green lazy daisy stitches on each half of the butterfly.

• Make a pink knot at the end of each loop.

28

Assembly

Use ¼-inch seam allowance and stitch right sides together unless otherwise indicated.

1. Cut out the embroidered butterfly. Position and pin right sides together on a piece of yellow for backing; trim to match embroidered butterfly edges.

2. Pin layered butterfly, backing side up, to batting scrap and stitch ¼ inch from the outside edges all around (Figure 12).

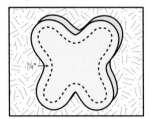

Figure 12

3. Cut a slash through the backing only. Apply seam sealant to the cut edges and let dry.

4. Turn the butterfly right side out through the slash. Press outer edges flat and handstitch opening closed.

5. Machine-stitch down the center of the butterfly to shape wings and as a beading guide (Figure 13).

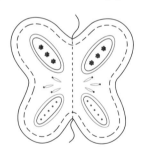

Figure 13

6. Stitch a running stitch through all the layers ³⁄₁₆ inch from the butterfly wing edges using 2 strands of black floss.

7. Use a backstitch beading technique to stitch 11 black beads down the middle of the wings along the machine-stitched line referring to the Stitch Guide on page 6.

Stitch Guide on page 6.

8. Apply glue to the center back of the butterfly and press to the box front at the upper right corner with butterfly flight design centered beneath the butterfly.

9. Fold the black wire in half and coil the ends outward with your fingers to shape the antennae (Figure 14).

Figure 14

10. Apply a dot of glue to the center of the antennae. Tuck antennae under the top center of the butterfly.

11. Sew the last bead to the top edge of the butterfly and into the box. ❖

Pretty & Practical Eyeglass Case

A padded eyeglass case will keep your specs safe and easy to find. Don't wear glasses? It would make a great storage case for a rotary cutter or a pair of scissors. The fly stitch is perfect for leaf centers and vines.

Finished Size
4 x 7 inches

Materials
- 8 x 7-inch piece red dot
- 8 x 10-inch piece muted black-and-white print
- 1¼ x 35-inch strip green dot
- 8 x 9-inch piece batting
- Stranded floss: green
- 3 (6mm) black beads
- Basic sewing supplies and equipment

Cutting

From red dot:
- Cut 2 (4 x 7-inch) back and front lining rectangles.
- Cut 3 (2¼-inch-diameter) circles for yo-yo flowers

From black-and-white print:
- Cut 1 (5 x 8-inch) front rectangle.
- Cut 1 (4 x 7-inch) back rectangle.

From green dot:
- Cut 1 each 1¼ x 5-inch and 1¼ x 30-inch binding strips.

From batting:
Cut 1 each 4 x 7-inch and 5 x 8-inch rectangles.

Embroidery
Refer to Embroidery Necessities on page 2 for stitching tips and the Stitch Guide on page 6. Full-size embroidery design and template are included on the insert.

1. Draw the eyeglass case front cutting lines on the 5 x 8-inch front rectangle. Use your preferred method to transfer the embroidery design onto the drawn shape.

2. Baste the 5 x 8-inch batting to the wrong side of the 5 x 8-inch marked case front and the 4 x 7-inch batting to the wrong side of a 4 x 7-inch lining rectangle.

3. Use 3 strands of green floss to embroider the eyeglass case front, stitching through the fabric and the batting as follows:

vine and leaf outlines	backstitch
leaf centers	fly stitch variation
vine line	fly stitch variation

4. Make yo-yo flowers using two strands of sewing thread and red dot circles and referring to Making Yo-Yos.

5. Bring matching sewing thread up through center of yo-yo. Pick up a bead and stitch back through center of yo-yo and embroidered design at a flower placement marked on the design (Figure 1). Take a second stitch through the flower, bead and case front. Knot and clip thread. Repeat with remaining flowers and beads.

Figure 1

Case Assembly

Use ¼-inch seam allowance and stitch right sides together unless otherwise indicated.

1. Cut out the case front on the marked cutting lines.

2. Use the eyeglass case front template to cut a front lining. Baste the embroidered front and front lining wrong sides together.

3. Press ¼ inch to the wrong side of one long edge of the 5-inch-long binding strip. Pin and stitch the opposite edge to the diagonal top edge of the case front (Figure 2); trim binding to match if necessary.

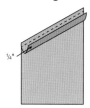

Figure 2

4. Fold the binding to the back, covering the machine stitches and slip stitch the folded edge to the lining.

Slip Stitch

5. Baste the case back and back lining, wrong sides together.

6. Position case front and back, lining sides together, matching side and bottom edges; baste.

7. Cut one short end of long binding strip at a 45-degree angle and press ¼ inch to the wrong side (Figure 3). Press ¼ inch to the wrong side of one long edge referring again to Figure 3.

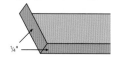

Figure 3

8. Starting about 3 inches from the folded short end, sew binding to case top edges, matching raw edges and using a ¼-inch seam. Stop stitching ¼ inch from corner and backstitch (Figure 4).

9. Bind the edges of the eyeglass case. Refer to Mitered Corner Binding on page 43 for binding tips. ❖

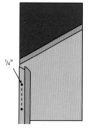

Figure 4

Making Yo-Yos

Using these simple instructions, you can make these easy floral-like embellishments for any sewing project.

1. Cut a circle the size indicated in cutting or assembly instructions.

2. Finger-press ¼ inch around the circle's outer edge to the wrong side. Hand-stitch in place around the circle taking a backstitch at the beginning to secure the thread as shown in Figure A.

Figure A

3. Gently pull the thread, tightly gathering the outer edge toward the center of the circle referring again to Figure A.

4. Knot the thread ends to secure the gathered edge and trim.

5. Flatten the circle with the gathered edge on the right side to complete the yo-yo as shown in Figure A.

6. Embellish and hand-stitch the completed yo-yo to the project as indicated in assembly instructions.

Upcycled Denim Maxi Tote

An item that is recycled to make something even better than the original is an upcycle! This maxi tote started out as a denim miniskirt, so it has lots of pockets. The blanket stitch is used to embellish and to attach the appliqués. Maxi-size, maxi-use, maxi-cute!

Finished Size
19 x 16 inches, without strap

Materials
- Woman's size 12 denim miniskirt
- 1 (12-inch) square each 2 coordinating multicolored prints
- ¼ yard coordinating multicolored print
- ⅛ yard green print
- ⅝ yard black print
- Size 5 pearl cotton:
  green
  colors to coordinate with fabrics
- 10 x 16-inch rectangle low loft batting
- 1 x 29½-inch strip fusible fleece
- 2 (1½-inch-wide) square rings
- 2 (1⅛-inch-diameter) black buttons
- 1 (24 x 36-inch) newsprint paper sheet
- Denim machine needle
- Walking or even-feed presser foot
- Basic sewing supplies and equipment

Cutting

From all multicolored prints:
- Cut a total of 7 circles: 2 (6-inch), 4 (5-inch) and 1 (4½-inch) in diameter for yo-yo flowers.

From multicolored print yardage:
- Cut 1 (3½ x 30-inch) strip for strap.

Embroidery
Refer to Embroidery Necessities on page 2 for stitching tips and the Stitch Guide on page 6. Full-size embroidery designs and template are included on the insert.

1. Determine the finished tote length. Trim skirt length to desired tote length plus ½ inch, measuring from the top edge of the waistband toward the hem line. Set aside cut-off portion. *Note: The skirt* *used to make the sample was 20 inches long. Desired length of finished tote is 16 inches. So the skirt was trimmed to 16½ inches, measuring from the top edge of the waistband and referring to Figure 1.*

Figure 1

Sizing Tip
The finished size of the tote is determined by the size of the skirt used. The 19 x 16-inch sample was made from a Woman's size 12 skirt. To make a smaller or larger tote, use a smaller or larger skirt and adjust amount of materials for lining accordingly.

2. Before completing the embroidery, make a lining pattern. Smooth out the skirt onto a large newsprint paper sheet with the side seams even and the front opening closed.

Sewing Tip
If you are concerned that the front opening may open when the tote is being used, machine-stitch it closed along the placket edge. No need to remove zippers or buttons.

3. Carefully trace the skirt from the lower edge of the waistband around to the opposite lower edge. Remove the skirt and draw a straight line

connecting the waistband points, referring to the red lines in Figure 2. Add a ½-inch seam allowance on all sides to traced shape.

Figure 2

4. Use the lining pattern to cut a front and back lining.

5. Transfer the curlicue vine embroidery design onto the front of the skirt using your preferred transfer method. ***Note:*** *A cardboard template or transfer paper works well on the heavy denim. Depending on the style of the skirt and pocket locations, you may have to alter the placement a little, unless you wish to embroider over the top of the pockets.*

6. Stitch the vines using 1 strand of green pearl cotton and a stem or outline stitch. ***Note:*** *Do not stitch into the pocket linings or stitch the front and back of the skirt together.*

7. Repeat steps 5 and 6 for the vines on the back of the skirt.

Flower & Leaf Embellishments

1. Refer to Making Yo-Yos on page 31 to make flowers.

2. Arrange and pin two large, two medium and one small yo-yo on the skirt front, referring to the project photo.

3. Use 1 strand of coordinating pearl cotton to blanket stitch through the yo-yo and the denim around the edge of the yo-yo, attaching each yo-yo to the skirt (Figure 3).

Figure 3

4. Arrange two medium yo-yos on the skirt back and attach, repeating step 3.

5. To make leaves, use template given on insert to trace six leaves ½ inch apart on the wrong side of one half of the green fabric. Fold the fabric in half, right sides together with shapes on top, and pin to batting (Figure 4).

Figure 4

6. Stitch around shapes on traced lines. Cut out each leaf ⅛ inch from seam. Trim the batting close to the seam. Clip the curves and trim the leaf tip.

7. Cut a slash through the top fabric only where indicated on pattern (Figure 5). Apply no-fray solution to the cut edges and let dry. Turn each leaf right side out through the slash. Hand-stitch the cut edges closed; press.

Figure 5

8. Using 1 strand of green pearl cotton, blanket stitch around each leaf.

9. Arrange and attach three leaves to the skirt front with a green running stitch down the leaf center, referring to the project photo and making five to six stitches on each leaf. ***Note:*** *The edges of the leaves are left free to give added dimension to the embellishments.*

10. Arrange and attach three leaves on the skirt back in the same manner, referring to photo of back of bag.

Assembly

Use a ½-inch seam allowance with right sides together unless otherwise indicated.

1. Turn the skirt inside out and sew the bottom edges together; press the seam open.

2. Fold and match the bottom seam to the side seam. Measure up 1 inch from the tip and draw a line perpendicular to the bottom seam to box the corner (Figure 6a).

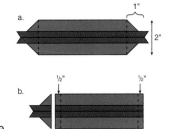

Figure 6

3. Stitch on the drawn line and trim the seam allowance to ½ inch (Figure 6b).
Note: Double-stitch or finish seam with a short, narrow zigzag stitch or serger to add strength to the bag corners.

4. Repeat steps 2 and 3 to box the opposite bag corner. Turn the bag right side out.

5. Repeat steps 1–4 with front and back lining. Do not turn right side out.

6. Press ½ inch to the wrong side of the lining top edge; set aside.

7. To make and attach the strap rings, cut two 3 x 6-inch strips from the reserved cut-off portion of the skirt.

8. Finish one long edge of one strip with a machine zigzag or overedge stitch or serger. Press unfinished long edge 1 inch to the wrong side. Press finished long edge over the raw edge almost meeting the fold (Figure 7). Topstitch ¼ inch along both folds. Repeat with second strip.

Figure 7

9. Thread the strip through the square ring and fold in half, wrong sides together and ends matching; baste ends together (Figure 8). Repeat with second ring.

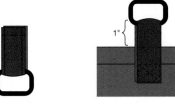

Figure 8   **Figure 9**

10. Position a strap ring unit on the wrong side of the waistband extending 1 inch above the top of the waistband. Referring to Figure 9, stitch a square with an X through the loop ends and a straight line along the top of the waistband through all layers. Repeat with second strap ring unit.

11. To make the strap, position fusible fleece on the wrong side of the 3½ x 30-inch fabric strip, 1 inch away from one long edge and ¼ inch away from the short ends (Figure 10). Follow manufacturer's instructions to fuse the fleece in place.

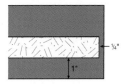

Figure 10

12. Fold and press the fabric short ends ¼ inch toward fleece. Fold 1 inch along long edge over fleece and press (Figure 11). Press ¼ inch of remaining long edge to wrong side and fold to match first fold. Topstitch ⅛ inch from all edges.

Figure 11

13. Thread one end of strap through a ring and fold end back 2½ inches; pin in place. Stitch a square with an X through all layers, referring to Figure 12. Repeat on other end of strap, being careful not to twist the strap.

Figure 12

14. Embellish strap ends by sewing a black button over stitching. ❖

Sew Tweet Fabric Bag

This sweet bag is embroidered with a little bird and heart motif featuring the satin stitch and padded satin stitch. It is lined and gathered with a satin ribbon and makes a beautiful gift or storage bag for small treasures.

Finished Size
9 x 13 inches

Materials
- Scraps light pink and yellow solids
- 12 x 11-inch piece white solid
- ⅓ yard or one fat quarter each soft green and yellow prints
- Stranded embroidery floss:

yellow	dark yellow
green	light green
pink	light pink
black	

- 42 inches ⅜-inch-wide yellow satin ribbon
- Scraps paper-backed fusible web
- Basic sewing supplies and equipment

Cutting

From soft green print:
- Cut 2 (2¼ x 5-inch) strips for A borders.
- Cut 1 (9½ x 3½-inch) strip for bottom border B.
- Cut 1 (9½ x 6-inch) rectangle for top border C.
- Cut 1 (9½ x 13½-inch) rectangle for bag back.

From yellow print:
- Cut 2 (9½ x 13½-inch) rectangles for lining front and back.

Embroidery
Refer to Embroidery Necessities on page 2 for stitching tips and the Stitch Guide on page 6. Full-size embroidery design is included on the insert.

1. Transfer the embroidery design to the center of the white rectangle using your preferred transfer method. *Note: Do not transfer the beak and small inner heart at this time.*

2. Embroider the design, as follows.

Use 3 strands embroidery floss to stitch:

Bird body, wing, tail feathers	yellow backstitch
Tail-feather end dots	dark yellow knots
Bird's eye	black satin stitch
Vine	green stem/ outline stitch
Outer heart	pink stem/outline stitch
Leaves	light green lazy daisy stitch
Flowers	light pink knot stitch
Bird's legs	black backstitch

3. For padded satin stitch, trace the small heart and beak onto the paper side of paper-backed fusible web scraps. Apply fusible web to wrong side of pink and yellow scraps following manufacturer's instructions. Cut out on pattern lines and remove the paper backing.

> ### Embroidery Tip
> *If desired, substitute a piece of fusible interfacing for the fusible web and fabric when preparing the padded satin stitch. Either method will provide a surface for the padded satin stitch, but the colored fabric is easier to see on a white background.*

4. Fuse the beak and heart in place following manufacturer's instructions and referring to the embroidery design. ***Note:*** *If you used an air- or water-soluble pen for the embroidery transfers, first remove all markings before using the iron on the design.*

5. Satin-stitch over the small heart shape with 3 strands of light pink floss. Outline the small heart with French or colonial knots made with 3 strands of light pink floss.

6. Satin-stitch over the beak using 3 strands of dark yellow floss.

38

Assembly

Use ¼-inch seam allowance and stitch right sides together unless otherwise indicated. Full-size templates are included on the insert.

1. Trim the embroidered piece to a 6 x 5-inch rectangle with the design centered.

2. Stitch the two A strips to opposite sides of the embroidered center; press seams toward A (Figure 1).

Figure 1

3. Stitch the B strip to the bottom of the pieced embroidery; press seam toward B (Figure 2).

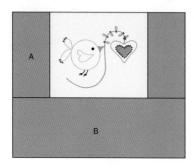

Figure 2

4. Stitch the C rectangle to the top of the pieced embroidery; press seam toward C (Figure 3).

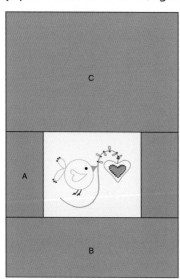

Figure 3

5. Pin the pieced bag front to the bag back and stitch the side and bottom edges. Leave a ⅝-inch-long opening on one side, starting 2¼ inches down from the top (Figure 4). Press seams open.

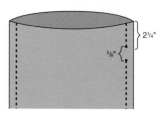

Figure 4

6. Fold and match the bottom seam to the side seam at one corner. Measure 1 inch from the corner tip and mark a line perpendicular to the side seam and stitch (Figure 5a). Trim seam allowance to ¼ inch, referring to Figure 5b. Repeat on second corner to box bag bottom.

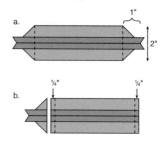

Figure 5

7. Press ¼ inch to wrong side of the top edge of the bag; turn the bag right side out.

8. Topstitch ⅛ inch from the ⅝ inch side seam opening on both sides to hold seam allowances open (Figure 6).

Figure 6

9. Pin front and back lining rectangles together, and stitch side and bottom edges.

10. Complete the lining, referring to steps 6 and 7. Do not turn right side out.

11. Insert the lining inside the bag, matching side seams; pin top edges together. Finish top edge by slip stitching folded edges together by hand or machine-topstitching close to the folded edges.

12. Machine-stitch two lines of stitches 1⅞ inches and 2¾ inches down from the top edge through bag and lining to make casing (Figure 7).

13. Insert ribbon through the casing and tie a knot on each ribbon end. ❖

Figure 7

Sew Tidy Sewing Machine Cover

Useful and pretty, this cover will keep harmful dust off your machine and brighten up your sewing corner at the same time. The embroidered sewing motifs decorate a pocket that can be used to store patterns, supplies or the machine cord. Cute little cross stitches fill in the background on the pocket.

Finished Size

Size of your machine

Materials

- 12-inch square white solid
- ¼ yard each green and red dot or coordinating print or solid
- 1⅛ yards multicolored print
- 12-inch square lightweight fusible interfacing
- 25 x 30-inch piece batting
- Stranded embroidery floss:

  blue   light blue   red
  orange   green   gray
  dark pink   purple   black
- 2 (¾-inch-diameter) cover button kits
- 2 size 4 snap sets
- Even-feed or walking presser foot (optional)
- Basic sewing supplies and equipment

Measuring Your Machine

Note: Be sure to include any knobs or other features that extend out from the machine body when measuring.

1. Measure the width of your machine from side to side at the widest point. _____

2. Measure the height from the bottom to the highest point. _____

3. Measure the depth from the front to the back at the widest point. _____

Cutting

From green dot:

- Cut 1 (1 x 7½-inch) pocket top border strip.
- Cut 2 (1 x 9-inch) pocket side border strips.
- Cut 1 (8½ x 9-inch) pocket lining rectangle.
- Cut 8 (4½ x 3-inch) side tab rectangles.
- Cut 2 (1½-inch-diameter) cover button circles.

From red dot:

- Cut 2½ x 42-inch binding strips to equal the perimeter of your cover plus 10 inches when joined.
- Cut 2 (4½-inch-diameter) yo-yo circles.

From multicolored print:

- Using the measurements taken for your machine, cut 2 [(machine width + 1½ inches) x (height + height + depth)] rectangles.

From the batting:

- Cut 1 (8½ x 9-inch) rectangle.
- Cut 1 rectangle the same size as the multicolored print rectangles.

Embroidery

Refer to Embroidery Necessities on page 2 for stitching tips and the Stitch Guide on page 6. Full-size embroidery design is included on the insert.

1. Fuse interfacing to wrong side of the white solid following the manufacturer's instructions. Transfer the embroidery design centered on the right side using your preferred transfer method.

2. Stitch the embroidery design using 2 strands of embroidery floss as follows:

Dress Form:
    Base   black stem/outline stitch
    Body form   blue stem/outline stitch

Scissors:
    Handles   orange stem/outline stitch
    Blades   gray stem/outline stitch
    Screw head   gray backstitch

Thread spools   gray backstitch
Thread   red and green stem/
                         outline stitch
Needle   gray stem/outline stitch
Buttons   purple, light blue and green
                         backstitch
Buttonholes   black knot stitch
Background   dark pink cross stitches

3. Complete pocket embroidery; press and trim to 7½ x 8½ inches with design centered.

Assembly

Use ¼-inch seam allowance and stitch right sides together unless otherwise indicated. Full-size templates are included on the insert.

1. Stitch the top pocket border strip to the embroidered pocket; press seam toward the border strip.

2. Stitch the pocket side border strips to opposite sides of embroidered pocket; press seams toward the borders.

3. Layer and pin the embroidered pocket and the pocket lining, right sides together, on the 8½ x 9-inch batting rectangle. Stitch sides and top, leaving bottom open. Trim batting close to seam and corners at an angle. Turn right side out; press. Baste bottom edges together ³⁄₁₆ inch from the edge (Figure 1).

Figure 1

4. Layer and pin together a cover rectangle, right side down; batting and second cover rectangle, right side up. Baste ³⁄₁₆ inch from all edges.

5. Pin pocket to right side of cover, 2 inches from the right side edge, matching raw bottom edges (Figure 2).

Figure 2

6. Stitch-in-the-ditch along the side borders, backstitching at top to secure (Figure 3).

Figure 3

7. To make side tabs, use the tab end trimming template provided to round off one short end of each tab rectangle.

8. Position and pin two tabs, right sides together, to a scrap of batting. Stitch all around, leaving open at short straight end (Figure 4). Trim batting close to seam line and clip curves. Turn right side out and press. Repeat to make a total of four tabs.

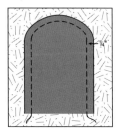

Figure 4

9. Pin the tabs to the lining side of the cover 4½ inches from the bottom and top edges, matching raw edges (Figure 5). Stitch in place.

Figure 5

10. Prepare and attach binding to cover rectangles referring to Mitered Corner Binding.

11. Prepare yo-yo flowers using 4½-inch-diameter circles referring to Making Yo-Yos on page 31.

12. Follow the manufacturer's directions to cover two buttons. Stitch a button to a yo-yo with the shank fitting into the center hole and then stitch the yo-yo to the right front tab end (Figure 6). Repeat with the second yo-yo and button, stitching to the left front tab.

Figure 6

13. Sew a snap set to the ends of the tabs, about 1 inch in from the rounded end, referring to Figure 7. ❖

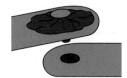

Figure 7

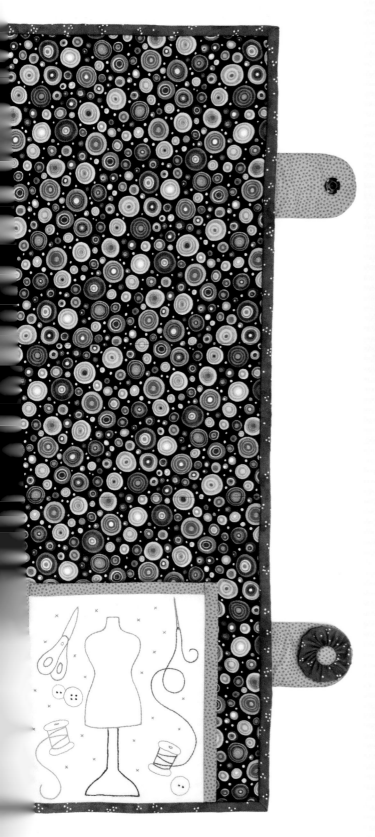

Mitered Corner Binding

• Join binding strips on short ends with diagonal seams to make one long strip; trim seams to ¼ inch and press seams open (Figure A).

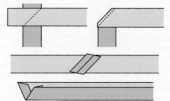

Figure A

• Fold 1 inch of one short end to wrong side and press. Fold the binding strip in half with wrong sides together along length, referring again to Figure A; press.

• Starting about 3 inches from the folded short end, sew binding to quilt top edges, matching raw edges and using a ¼-inch seam. Stop stitching ¼ inch from corner and backstitch (Figure B)

Stop ¼"

Figure B

• Fold binding up at a 45-degree angle to seam and then down even with quilt edges, forming a pleat at corner, referring to Figure C.

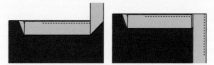

Figure C

• Resume stitching from corner edge as shown in Figure C, down quilt side, backstitching ¼ inch from next corner. Repeat, mitering all corners, stitching to within 3 inches of starting point.

• Trim binding end long enough to tuck inside starting end and complete stitching (Figure D).

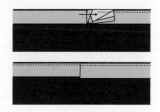

• Fold binding to quilt back and stitch in place by hand or machine to complete your quilt.

Figure D

Stitch Sampler

A sampler is a very traditional form of journaling the stitches learned and, at the same time, creating a handcrafted piece of art worthy of hanging on the wall to admire. This is a fun mini sampler showcasing the 10 stitches from the book. Feel free to add more stitch variations and make it your own. And be sure to sign it in stitches!

Finished Size
13 x 17 inches

Materials
- Scrap of red solid
- ⅓ yard white solid
- ½ yard black with white dots
- Size 8 black pearl cotton
- Stranded embroidery floss:

blue	light blue	dark blue
black	green	dark green
gray	orange	variegated pink
pink	purple	red
yellow		

- 6 size 8/0 red seed beads
- ¼ yard lightweight fusible interfacing
- 13½ x 17½-inch batting
- Scrap fusible web
- 6 (¾-inch-diameter) white buttons
- 2 (¾-inch) plastic rings

Cutting

From white solid:
- Cut 3 (12-inch) squares.

From black with white dots:
- Cut 8 (1½ x 3½-inch), 5 (1½ x 13½-inch) and 2 (1½ x 17½) sashing/border strips.
- Cut 1 (13½ x 17½-inch) backing rectangle.

From lightweight interfacing:
Cut 12 (3½-inch) squares.

Embroidery
Refer to Embroidery Necessities on page 2 for stitching tips and the Stitch Guide on page 6. The embroidery is marked and stitched four squares at a time for easier handling. Full-size embroidery designs are included on the insert.

1. On the right side of each white square, measure and draw four 3½-inch squares, leaving a 1-inch space between the squares (Figure 1).

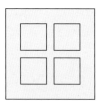

Figure 1

2. Fuse an interfacing square inside the drawn squares to the back of the fabric following the manufacturer's instructions. ***Note:*** *If necessary, use a light box or hold the fabric up to a window to line up the interfacing.*

3. Transfer an embroidery design to each of the squares using your preferred transfer method.

4. Stitch the embroidery in each square as desired referring to the labeled embroidery designs. ***Note:*** *In each sampler square, the featured stitch is worked at the top using black pearl cotton. The variations are worked with 2 or 3 strands of floss in assorted colors referring to the design or as desired.*

5. Complete all embroidery and cut out each block on the drawn lines.

Sampler Assembly
Use ¼-inch seam allowance and stitch right sides together unless otherwise indicated.

1. Arrange the 12 embroidered squares into four rows of three blocks each (Figure 2).

Figure 2

2. Place one 1½ x 3½-inch sashing strip between the squares (Figure 3). Stitch blocks and sashing into rows; press seams toward sashing strips.

Figure 3

3. Position a 1½ x 13½-inch sashing strip between each row and at the top and bottom. Stitch the rows and sashing strips together (Figure 4); press seams toward sashing strips.

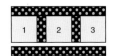

Figure 4

4. Stitch a 1½ x 17½-inch border strip to each side; press seams toward borders.

5. Layer embroidered sampler top, right side up, and backing, right side down, on the batting rectangle. Stitch all around, leaving a 5-inch opening on the bottom edge. Trim batting close to seam and trim corners at an angle. Turn right side out through opening.

6. Fold opening seam allowance to inside and press the edges flat. Hand-stitch the opening closed using a slip stitch and matching thread.

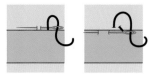

Slip Stitch

7. Stitch-in-the-ditch between the borders and the pieced center, referring to Figure 5.

Figure 5

8. Sew a white button through all the layers at the intersection of the vertical and horizontal sashing strips, referring to the sampler photo.

9. Sew a plastic ring to each top back corner of the sampler for hangers (Figure 6). ❖

Figure 6

Sources

Annie's
(800) 282-6643
AnniesCatalog.com
Fabric, needles, iron-on transfer pens,
FriXion pens, water- and air-soluble pens,
Sulky Cotton Petites and other supplies

Colonial Patterns Inc
(816) 471-3313
www.colonialpatterns.com
Aunt Martha's Stitch 'em Up Kitchen Towels

DMC
(800) 275-4117
www.dmc-usa.com
Stranded embroidery floss, pearl cotton, needles

Presencia
(800) 963-3353
www.presenciaamerica.com
Stranded embroidery floss, Finca Perlé Cotton, needles

For more inspiration and guidance in learning embroidery stitches and their countless variations, author Chris Malone suggests two classic books, both of which have been revised and reprinted:

The Stitches of Creative Embroidery
by Jacqueline Enthoven
Revised and reprinted by Schiffer Publishing in 1987

Mary Thomas's Dictionary of Embroidery Stitches
Updated by Jan Eaton and reprinted by Trafalgar Square Books in 1998

Annie's *Easy to Learn Hand Embroidery* is published by Annie's, 306 East Parr Road, Berne, IN 46711. Printed in USA. Copyright © 2014 Annie's.
All rights reserved. This publication may not be reproduced in part or in whole without written permission from the publisher.

RETAIL STORES: If you would like to carry this pattern book or any other Annie's publication, visit AnniesWSL.com.

Every effort has been made to ensure that the instructions in this pattern book are complete and accurate. We cannot, however, take responsibility for human error, typographical mistakes or variations in individual work. Please visit AnniesCustomerCare.com to check for pattern updates.

ISBN: 978-1-59635-970-3
1 2 3 4 5 6 7 8 9

Photo Index

11

15

40

18

21

22

24

29

33

36

44